ESTHER

OTHER POETRY BOOKS
BY JOHN PIPER

The Innkeeper
The Misery of Job and the Mercy of God
The Prodigal's Sister
Ruth
Velvet Steel

ESTHER

JOHN PIPER

Paintings by Glenn Harrington

WHEATON, ILLINOIS

Esther

Copyright © 2012 by Desiring God Foundation

Published by Crossway
         1300 Crescent Street
         Wheaton, Illinois 60187

Cover and interior paintings: Glenn Harrington, Shannon Associates

Cover design: Josh Dennis

Interior design and typesetting: Kevin Lipp

First printing 2012

Printed in China

Scripture quotations are from the ESV® Bible (*The Holy Bible, English Standard Version*®), copyright © 2001 by Crossway. Used by permission. All rights reserved.

All emphases in Scripture quotations have been added by the author.

Hardcover: 978-1-4335-3418-8

PDF ISBN: 978-1-4335-3419-5

Mobipocket ISBN: 978-1-4335-3420-1

ePub ISBN: 978-1-4335-3421-8

Library of Congress Cataloging-in-Publication Data
Piper, John, 1946-
Esther / John Piper ; illustrated by Glenn Harrington.
   p. cm.
  ISBN 978-1-4335-3418-8 (hc)
  1. Esther, Queen of Persia—Poetry. I. Title.
PS3566.I59E88   2012
811'.54—dc23   2012007327

Crossway is a publishing ministry of Good News Publishers.

WHAT'S BEHIND THIS POEM?

Every Advent season for twenty-seven years I wrote narrative poems as a kind of Christmas gift to the church I pastor. *Esther* is one of those gifts.

I have loved poetry since I was a teenager. It has always seemed plain to me that the imagination is a gift of God and is meant to reflect his own creativity. He thought up the universe out of nothing, then created us in his own image. So we do that kind of thing. Not that *very* thing. But that *kind* of thing. Only God creates out of nothing. We are not God. But we are like him when we create.

Perhaps this is why I feel so at home when writing poetry. I don't mean I feel relaxed or in control. I usually don't. I mean: This is who I am—who God made me to be. A creator, a maker. I suspect that deep down that's the way we all feel when we are making what God made us to make. A poem is not necessarily a better thing to make than a birthday cake, or a rose garden, or a website. But it is one of the things I love to make.

What I mean by poetry is this: "An effort to share a moving experience by using language that is chosen and structured differently from ordinary prose." Sometimes it rhymes. Sometimes it doesn't. Sometimes it has a regular cadence. Sometimes it doesn't. But almost always the poet has experienced something—something horrible or wonderful or ordinary—and he feels that he must share it. Using words differently from ordinary prose is his way of trying to awaken something of this experience (and more) in the reader.

～

When I read the Bible, I experience God. This is the astonishing power and dignity God has given to his Word. He meets us there. "The LORD revealed *himself* to Samuel at Shiloh by the *word* of the LORD" (1 Sam. 3:21). This is amazing. We meet God *himself* by the Word.

And when we do, we are affected. It may be terror, or it may be ecstasy, or it may be an inexpressible peace. But for poets, at least, experiencing something *inexpressible* does not mean silence. It's precisely the *inexpressible something* that poetry is meant to help us see or feel. If it were merely expressible— if there were nothing ineffable about it—there would be no need for a poem. But everywhere in the Bible we meet reality that exceeds our comprehension. We must find a way to at least point or suggest or hint. It's too wonderful—or too something—to keep to ourselves.

So it is with the book of Esther. This book never mentions God. But he is everywhere—the invisible hand that moves empires for the sake of his people. The invisibility of his name in the book is a pointer to the invisibility of his majestic rule in history. Human designs are inexorably undone. And the way God turns the tables is breathtaking.

The king can't sleep. So someone reads to him the royal records of "memorable deeds." All of this just so that

Haman, the arrogant Jew hater, by a fluke encounter, would be forced to honor Mordecai—the Jew (chapter 6). Such things are everywhere in this book. The invisible God is everywhere behind them. Just as he was at Golgotha.

I won't try to say in this introduction what moved me most in reading Esther. That's what the poem is for. But I will say how I go about it. I retell the story by filling in possibilities of what might have been, mingled with what really was. My aim is to respect what really was by creating nothing that could not have been. Nothing has been changed in the biblical story. And what has been created is not Scripture. It is meant to awaken us to the wonder of what is really there. Here are some historical facts that we know:

- The kingdom of Babylon fell before Cyrus the Persian in 539 BC. The people of Israel had, by that time, been in captivity in Babylon for decades.

- In 538 BC, Cyrus decreed that the Jews could return to their homeland.

- Ahasuerus reigned as king of Persia from 485 to 464 BC.

- Esther became queen in Persia about the year 479 BC.

- Susa, where the story of the book of Esther takes place, was the capital of the Persian Empire and lay about 350 miles southeast of Babylon.

- Esther was Mordecai's cousin, "the daughter of Abihail the uncle of Mordecai" (Est. 2:15). "She had neither father nor mother" (Est. 2:7).

- Mordecai was "the son of Jair, son of Shimei, son of Kish, a Benjaminite" (Est. 2:5). I have treated Abihail and Jair as brothers and both as the sons of Shimei, who would then be Esther's grandfather. Shimei was thus old enough to have been among the Babylonian captives. I treat him as not returning to Palestine but dreaming of some destiny in Persia.

- Nabonidus was the last king of Babylon and was defeated by Cyrus the Persian.

- Borsippa was a city about twelve miles southwest of Babylon.

- Nippur was a neighboring city along with its surrounding region.

- Opis was the Babylonian city where Nabonidus made his last stand against the Persians.

- Hadassah was Esther's Jewish name (Est. 2:7), which means "myrtle."

These are the historical realities I try to honor in my retelling of Esther's story. Don't get bogged down trying to figure out genealogies. Let the story carry you forward.

Perhaps a short comment on reading poetry would be helpful. Beware of thinking the line breaks signal pauses or emphases. They don't. They will do their best work for you if you ignore them. Only pause when there is a punctuation mark. This way the stilted sound we associate with bad poems (ta-DA ta-DA ta-DA ta-DA, pause, ta-DA ta-DA ta-DA) will be, happily, avoided. There is a cadence that matters. But its effect will be felt most if it is read and heard effortlessly and unself-consciously.

I read recently that one well-known English teacher tells his students that we must rid ourselves of the notion that poems can be made sense of in a single reading.

That's probably true. It takes one or two times through to discover even *how* it should be read, let alone what it means. When the cadence is caught, and the wording is familiar, the stroll through the poem does not require much attention to the path, and you can lift up your eyes to the vistas.

I must stop. I've perhaps already said too much. Poems are poems. They should stand pretty much on their own. I hope you enjoy *Esther.*

*F*ar east of ruined Palestine

The year five hundred thirty-nine

Was filled with hope. The western sun

Set once for all on Babylon;

And Nabonidus fell before

The Persian forces at the door

Of Opis. Mighty Cyrus, king

Of Persia, set his signet ring

Upon the seal of victory,

And published in his first decree

That Jews could now return to live

Again in Jacob's land, and give

Themselves to serve the living God.

But there were some who took the rod

Of God's chastisement so to heart

That now their faith and hope would chart

Another course: at least one clan

Within the tribe of Benjamin,

The clan of Shimei, would stay

In pagan Babylon and pray

That now, and generations hence,

God might, in gracious providence,

Be pleased to use them for some great

And saving work—to penetrate,

Perhaps, some curse beyond the bounds

Of Israel, with joyful sounds

Of sovereign love.

$\mathcal{S}$ome forty years

Of hope and prayer and frequent tears

Went by in Babylon. One night

A million brilliant stars sang bright

Against the sable Persian sky,

And called the agèd Shimei

To climb the ancient cliffs beside

The dark Euphrates, up the pride

Of Borsippa. With Abihail

His youngest son he took the trail

That led to Nippur Ridge, and stood

There with a woolen traveller's hood

Hung halfway on his snowy head.

And facing to the east he said,

I had a dream, my son, that some

Day what we've longed to see will come,

Not here, but even farther east,

And that for you and me, at least,

The promise that the Lord has planned

Is not found in the Promised Land.

But I am old, and so the dream

Is yours, my son. And if it seem

Too slow, doubt not the faithfulness

Of God; one generation lives

And dies to serve the next; he gives

A glimpse to Moses 'cross the vale,

And me tonight. But, Abihail,

Tomorrow take your wife, though she

Is great with child and frailty,

And set your face toward Susa where

The king sits on his throne; and there

Beyond the Tigris serve the Lord

Of hosts, and wait until the cord

Of providence is woven full.

Then God will set his heel, and pull

The powers of the world into

The service of his love for you,

And for his children scattered through

The empire. Yes! Mark now, and do

As I have said. God will provide

For you, doubt not, and for your bride,

And for the child. Be strong, my son,

You will not be alone. The one

Who governs dreams, and gives

Us everything we need, and lives

On ev'ry inch of ground we tread,

Will be with you. You will be led;

And lest you feel alone, he spoke

These words, 'My soul will not revoke

The promise I have made. Go now,

My chosen, Abihail. My vow

And pledge is this: that with you I

Will send your nephew, Mordecai.'"

*T*he pretty girl sat on the floor

Beside the fire and said once more

To Mordecai, "Abba, how did

My mother die? You haven't hid

Such things from me for all these years;

And late at night I see the tears

Roll down your cheek, and I must feel

That it would help if we could kneel

Before the Lord and bear this thing

Together. You and I could sing,

Then, eye to eye about the ways

Of God. And wouldn't those dark days

Reveal the same God that you've taught

Me these twelve years to trust? And ought

I not to know then, Mordecai,

How both my parents came to die?"

The road from here to Babylon

Is hard, Hadassah. It's not fun,

And even less if you're a Jew.

And we were three—or four, with you.

Three hundred miles of sweat and hate.

And you were big and three weeks late.

And no one gave us room. The heat

Was indescribable. Her feet

Were swollen, scarlet hot. He prayed,

Your father, Abihail, for shade.

That's all! Not for a house or nurse,

Or stream or birthing stool or purse

To bribe the keepers of the inn.

Just shade! And just in time (we thought)

There was a myrtle tree. She fought,

But you were big and she was thin,

And there was blood, and we were men . . . . "

*D*id mother ever hold me—once?"

*Y*es, right away! And your response

Was perfect peace. I wish that I

Could tell you what she said, but my

Heart moved me back as Abihail

Knelt down to kiss your mother's pale

And sweaty face and stroke your hair.

I couldn't hear what happened there,

And Abihail would never say

Too much. Just this: 'The myrtle was

A gift of God. Jehovah does

What he must do. But there was shade!

And we agreed, the girl is made

To be a myrtle, comfort, shield.

And so together there we sealed

Her name: Hadassah in the tongue

Of Israel. May she be sung

In festival for centuries

To come.'

Alone and on his knees

Your father dug her grave beneath

The myrtle tree, and pushed the dirt

In with his own strong hands. The hurt,

As you may guess, was deeper than

The grave. We prayed and then we ran

With you. God led us to a house,

And we besought the farmer's spouse

For mercy and a nurse. 'You're Jews,'

She said, 'Perhaps my man could use

A few "employees" for a spell.

Whose kid is this?' 'She's mine, you tell

Your husband I will work his farm

If you can keep this child from harm.'

For two long years, Hadassah, we

Were Jewish slaves, but you were free

From harm, and grew up like a tree

Beside the brook of loyalty—

The loyalty of God to his

Design. He never doubted this,

Your father, Abihail, I mean.

The tree of hope stayed ever green

That Shimei had planted in

His heart. And neither pain nor sin

Nor death could break the fibers of

His mighty faith: that sovereign love

Would somehow take your mother's death,

His father's dream, your living breath,

And weave them with some loving lace

Into a tapestry of grace.

I've never known a stronger man

Than Abihail, your father."

*C*an

You tell me, Abba, what became

Of him? To me he's just a name.

But I would like to know him, see

His face, his hope, especially

The dream."

He worked himself so thin

That when the fever came, his skin

Hung on his bones like dough. I nursed

Him to the end. He never cursed

A soul, not one, alive or dead,

But near the end looked up and said,

'Could you please take me, Mordecai,

Down to the myrtle tree to die?'

I laid him by your mother's grave,

And waited through the night. He gave

His final thought for you: once more

He whispered motionless, 'Before

I die give me your word, my friend,

To bring her to the journey's end,

To Susa, as my father dreamed.

For it must be that God has deemed

For you and for Hadassah there

To see the answer to our prayer.'

He took my hand, 'Swear, Mordecai,

As long as there's a Persian sky,

You will not take Hadassah back

To Israel. And if you lack

For anything, then perish if

You must, but not beside the cliff

Of Borsippa or Jordan stream.

Forsake not, Mordecai, the dream

Of Shimei and Abihail.

The plan of God can never fail.

We have not followed him in vain.'

You see, Hadassah, even pain

Could not suffice to break the hope

Of Abihail, or dim the scope

Of his design for you. I took

You yet that night, and we forsook

The shame of slavery and came

To Susa. Here another name

I gave to you to make your way

As easy as I could. They say

That *Esther* means 'a brilliant star.'"

I thank you, Abba. Ten years are

A lot of love for fathering

A cousin."

Esther, let us sing

Now, like you said, together eye

To eye. The God who made the sky

And rules the earth with awesome might,

Is wielding all the world this night

To bring this story to an end

Beyond our power to comprehend."

At thirty-five her hair was fine
And cinder black. Nor was there sign
Of aging in her queenly face.
And those who saw the tiny trace
Of tragedy left in her eyes,
Compared it to the Persian skies
When storms have purged the gloomy air,
And left the faintest rainbow there.

She gave her firstborn son the name
Of Abihail, and hoped the flame
Of faith would burn in him, as pure
And bright as once burned deep and sure
Within her father's breast.

*O*ne night

The boy said, "Mamma, am I right

That you became the queen because

You were so beautiful? And laws

Were changed because you were so brave?"

*Q*ueen Esther smiled, "Can you behave

If I let you stay up a while?

If so, we'll put another pile

Of logs into the fire, and I

Will tell you, Abihail, just why

Your mommy is the Queen of all

The land—from Egypt to the tall

And snowy Himalayas."

I'll

Behave," he said, and tried to smile

And look as wide awake as he

Could look for being five. "And we

Can sit here by the fire," he said,

"And later I can go to bed

When you're all through. Okay?"

*W*e'll see,"

She said (the way moms do). "Could be

We'll need another night, you know.

We can't talk till the roosters crow!"

And so they stoked the fire once more,

And Esther shut the royal door,

And Abihail climbed in her lap,

And nestled with his little cap

Beneath her royal chin.

*Y*our great-

Grandfather had a dream: 'Now wait

No more in Babylon,' a voice

From heaven said, 'But come, rejoice,

For God has made a plan to save

His people through your son. A slave

Will turn the powers of unbelief

Upon their heads, and all the grief

Of captive Israel will turn

To joy.' Of course, we had to learn,

In time, that what the dream had meant

Was that, though Abihail was sent—

The son of Shimei—'twas I

And your good uncle Mordecai

Would come at God's appointed time,

And block the hate-filled, bloody crime

Of Haman."

Mommy, he was bad."

I'll tell you, Abihail, the sad
And ugly truth: Indeed he was
A wicked man. A coward does
A lot of sneaky things to make
Himself look good when he's a fake.
And Haman even tried to bring
Ten thousand talents to the king,
And all in silver, if the Jews
Could all be caught and killed. And why?
Because he hated Mordecai!"

$\mathcal{B}$ut, Mommy, Mordecai is good."

$\mathcal{I}$ndeed he is! And solid wood,

My son, makes rotten timber rage.

The wicked Haman in his cage

Of cowardice could not abide

The freedom of the man outside."

"And did the king, my dad, agree?"

Sometimes, dear Abihail, we see

Things different than they are, and make

What later seems a big mistake.

He did agree. But God did not

Allow success for Haman's plot,

Nor of the king's decree. It seems

That this is what the noble dreams

Of Shimei were all about,

And why my father didn't doubt.

God had a plan to save the Jews

From Haman's wicked scheme: to use

Not Shimei, nor Abihail,

Nor mighty armies to assail

The Persian palace walls, but me,

A Jewish orphan girl, to free

The sons of Israel from death.

And even now it takes my breath

Away to think about the ways

Of God, and how from ancient days

He planned it all, and ruled the world,

Right down to how my hair was curled,

When all the girls were gathered for

The king to see, and what I wore,

And how I walked, and everything

It took to cause a Persian king

To choose from all the women in

The world this exiled Jewish kin

Of Shimei. O, Abihail!

I hope you see, and never fail

To know that there's a God in charge

Of all the world. He governs large

And small. He sets up kings to reign,

And takes the lion by the mane.

None moves without the Lord's command,

And none can stay his mighty hand."

*B*ut, Mommy, weren't you ever scared?"

*Y*es, Abihail, but God prepared
A special gift for me one night:
He showed me that by doing right
And trusting him, there would be less
To lose and more to gain! And yes,
Should I have even lost my life,
It would be true: to be the wife
Of Persia's king, and false to God,
Is no reward. What good to trod
A bridge of gold above a flood
Of icy hate and Jewish blood?"

What did you do to save the Jews?"

Your uncle Mordecai sent news
To me about the king's decree,
And said that I should try to see
The king, and tell him I'm a Jew.
And even when your uncle knew
That I could lose my life this way,
He said, 'If on this dark'ning day
You hold your tongue, God will provide
Protection from some other side,
And you will die. But, Esther, think:
Is not there now some holy link
Of precious providence between
The Jewish plight and who is queen?'

And so your uncle Mordecai

Filled me with hope. 'If I must die

Then I will die,' your mother said."

The sleepy prince picked up his head

And asked, "Did Daddy change his mind?"

I'd rather say, God touched the blind,"

The queen replied. "You see, dear son,

If you would truly know what's done

Upon the earth, you have to ask:

What power is hid behind the mask

Of man's design? Am I the queen

Because of looks? What does it mean

That Haman hung on gallows made

For Mordecai, and that the blade

Aimed at the Jews, instead of these

Was thrust against their enemies?"

*B*ut Abihail was breathing deep,

And soon the lad would be asleep.

So Esther closed his drooping eyes

And prayed that God would make him wise.

And then she sang a lullaby

That she had learned from Mordecai:

There once was a baby born under a tree,

Her dear mamma died, and nobody could see,

Her daddy knelt down by her side on his knee,

And no one but God knew what this girl would be.

Her branches spread out and their beauty was seen,

The shade that she made was a deep myrtle green,

An orphan and lovely as she turned eighteen,

And no one but God knew: Tomorrow a queen.

est well, my precious Abihail,

When you are weak, God will prevail.

Trust now the Lord your soul to keep,

He rules the nations while you sleep."

Now listen, children, young and old,

God multiplies ten thousandfold

The little power that we bring.

He makes our winter weakness sing

Of his full summer's strength, and burns

The rags of shame to ashes, turns

The course of human history, blocks

The haughty schemes of strutting cocks,

And brings the prophecies of men

To naught. And rising up, he then,

Against all high conspiracies,

And proud imperial machines,

Makes orphans into kings and queens.